Words Of Wisdom

100 Acrostics on Values, Virtues and Blessings

Rhodesia

Ukiyoto Publishing

All global publishing rights are held by

Ukiyoto Publishing

Published in 2022

Content Copyright © Rhodesia

ISBN 9789360162719
*All rights reserved.
No part of this publication may be reproduced,
transmitted, or stored in a retrieval system, in any
form by any means, electronic, mechanical,
photocopying, recording or otherwise, without the
prior permission of the publisher.*

The moral rights of the authors have been asserted.

*This book is sold subject to the condition that it shall
not by way of trade or otherwise, be lent, resold,
hired out or otherwise circulated, without the
publisher's prior consent, in any form of binding or
cover other than that in which it is published.*

www.ukiyoto.com

Dedication

This book is wholeheartedly dedicated to all the readers, and to the author's loved ones - late father Rudy, mother Evelyn, sister Rudilyn, children Liana and Rodemil, friends, and beloved. The help of Dr. Jazzie Burgos in introducing the publishing company to the author is highly-appreciated.

Contents

Prologue	1
Be	3
Active	4
Calm	5
Clean	6
Confident	7
Content	8
Diligent	9
Fair	10
Fulfilled	11
Generous	12
Gentle	13
Good	14
Grateful	15
Happy	16
Healthy	17
Holy	18
Honest	19
Humble	20
Kind	21

Loyal	22
Meek	23
Noble	24
Open	25
Patient	26
Present	27
Proper	28
Prudent	29
Pure	30
Punctual	31
Ready	32
Resilient	33
Right	34
Still	35
True	36
Do	37
Ask	38
Care	39
Channel	40
Comfort	41
Create	42

Endure	43
Flow	44
Focus	45
Forgive	46
Grow	47
Heal	48
Hear	49
Help	50
Inspire	51
Know	52
Laugh	53
Learn	54
Plan	55
Praise	56
Pray	57
Respect	58
Save	59
Seek	60
Share	61
Smile	62
Strive	63

Succeed	64
Thank	65
Transcend	66
Trust	67
Value	68
Work	69
Workship	70
Have	71
Abundance	72
Awe	73
Beauty	74
Courage	75
Discipline	76
Faith	77
Family	78
Freedom	79
Friend	80
Glory	81
Grit	82
Harmony	83
Heart	84

Home	85
Hope	86
Humor	87
Integrity	88
Joy	89
Legacy	90
Light	91
Life	92
Longevity	93
Love	94
Mercy	95
Mission	96
Paradise	97
Peace	98
Prosperity	99
Serenity	100
Strength	101
Temperance	102
Victory	103
Vision	104
Wisdom	105

About the Author 106

Prologue

Beloved Reader,

To you I dedicate and share this book of the gifts of spirit, a meager sampling that is, since all the infinite spiritual gifts cannot be encapsulated in merely 100 poems. May these words serve like trails on our path, that we may trace back to return home, where love and peace reside.

The poems are in the form of acrostics, that is, the beginning of every line form a word, which is the theme of the poem. This book is thus a book of acrostics, revolving around virtues, values and blessings - the priceless treasures I would like to share and perpetuate to the world. All these are packed in words, mere words, which can shed light and convey so much meaning and wisdom.

There are three sections - Be, Do, Have, separating the adjectives, verbs, and nouns. Be, Do, Have is also a principle that states we should embody character first, then execute, before we achieve our goals. It is actually a cycle, for after having achieved a spiritual goal we become a greater version of ourselves. We expand as our souls learn and mature in the short span of time that we are given in this lifetime.

All of us in our own unique ways contribute to the expansion of the universal soul maturity. I hope this book may be able to fulfill this contribution in our life journey.

With deepest love and prayers,

Rhodesia

Be

Become the person you wish to be
Embody your wished for quality.

Active

Aspire a useful life,

Catalyze a needed change,

Tract a newfound path,

Initiate development,

Volunteer in worthwhile cause,

Energize the course you chose.

Calm

Composed in chaos,
Able to manage,
Lull any damage,
Motion may cause.

Clean

Clear as crystal,
Litter-free soul,
Every inch spotless,
Angelic core,
Neat overall.

Confident

Confront challenges,
Obstacles and tests,
Negotiate needs,
Face utmost fears.
Implement with fierce
Dreams deeply set.
Eye contact, chin up,
Never cower,
Trust your power.

Content

Calmly rest the cares,
On greater might,
Nothing will disturb
The peace of mind.
Enveloped in joy,
No need for things,
Truly rich and unwanting.

Diligent

Do your work with all you heart,
Instill value in every second.
Like the tireless labor of tiny ants,
Inspire others with your example.
Great accomplishments await,
Every finished task is worth,
Nothing feels more gratifying
Than at the end of day, you are fulfilling.

Fair

Favor all or none at all,
Advantage for the whole,
In accord to moral rules,
Reason and justice call.

Fulfilled

Finished task,
Unified ends,
Legacy outlast
Family and friends.
Inspiration shines
Like sun at dawn,
Life lived divine,
Excellence shown
Deserves renown.

Generous

Giving more,
Extending help,
Noble chore
Enriches life.
Ready to serve,
Overdeliver,
Unselfishly
Share to others.

Gentle

Gestures soft and soothing,
Endearing and forbearing,
Neither harsh nor too strong,
Tender, touching like a song,
Light and soft like the lamb,
Ever pleasing to succumb.

Good

Genuine kindness
Overcomes sadness,
Overshadows darkness,
Delivers gladness.

Grateful

Greet each day with a smile,
Remember events worthwhile,
Appreciate the value of all things.
Thank the Almighty for blessing
Every unspoken need or wanting
Freely furnished without counting,
Unconditionally granting
Light, love and life in living.

Happy

Heavenly bliss,
Affectionate smile,
Perfect peace,
Pleasant while,
Youthful heart.

Healthy

Heed your body,
Empower your engine,
Attend to your system,
Live long and fully.
Treat yourself well,
Hold yourself accountable,
You are your priceless wealth.

Holy

Heaven's gates open
Over those who knock,
Left their past person
Yonder to please God.

Honest

Heart of honor
Offered in earnest,
Needless to hinder
Escape of candor,
Sincere in rightness,
Truthful at all times.

Humble

Handling offenses gracefully,
Uncoupling pride and problem,
Mending rift is priority,
Beyond nursing self-esteem.
Low-key despite achievements,
Enabling others' viewpoint.

Rhodesia

Kind

Keenly attuned to others
In heart, words, and deeds,
No second thoughts in serving
Destitute people their needs.

Loyal

Legions of angels
Obey a commander,
Yearning a cause for
Absolute surrender,
Least to turn away.

Meek

Modest and gentle
Even when provoked,
Enduring injury
Knowing how to cope.

Noble

Noteworthy and lofty
Objectives and ideals,
Bestowing quality
Least likely compromised,
Exalted in morals.

Open

Operate from a free space,
Possibilities are endless,
Encourage and accept,
New ideas and concepts.

Patient

Prolonged vexation,
Abated aspiration,
Time in suspension.
Irritation averted,
Endurance practiced,
Nuisance tempered.
Troubles tolerated.

Present

Place your whole being,
Reside in the now,
Everything's unraveling,
Synchronized somehow,
Enjoy the moment,
Nurture each event,
Today is a gift.

Proper

Putting matters to perspective,
Relative to a situation,
Overseeing and selective,
Placed in suitable condition,
Excluding accordingly,
Regarding morality.

Prudent

Prepared for future,
Rehearsed to gauge,
Unerring measure,
Disciplined sage.
Exact decision with
Necessary caution
Thwart dire situation.

Pure

Prim plus proper,
Untainted and clear,
Refined with utmost care,
Exempted from smear.

Punctual

Prepare early,
Use time wisely,
Never be late,
Cause deals to wait,
Time spells wealth,
Utter respect,
Arrive ahead,
Lead in good stead.

Ready

Rehearse in mind,
Easy to find,
Adverse or fine,
Devise a plan,
Yielding triumph.

Resilient

Rebound soon,
Escape the gloom.
Start a new
Indestructible you.
Live again
In spite of pain,
End your sadness,
Nurse your heartaches,
Today is your rebirth.

Right

Remember the laws
Inscribed in scriptures,
Good to follow,
Holy and pure,
Totally proper.

Still

Stay strong and silent
Through turbulent times,
Instill calm surrender,
Lie low amid the storm,
Let it pass, while you remain.

True

To live and speak what's
Real and genuine,
Unpretentious
Essence wins.

Do

Direct your volition
Oblige task completion.

Ask

Answers come when questioned,
Seekers find treasures,
Knowledge can be summoned.

Care

Cherish,
Attend,
Remember
Every moment.

Channel

Choose your path,
Harness the energy -
Anger, fear, or wrath,
Neither yield blindly
Nor bottle up miserly,
Employ the driving force,
Leverage to worthy course.

Comfort

Console from grief,
Ordeal and pain,
Mitigate harm,
Free from constraint.
Oasis of care,
Restore the unwell,
Take away despair.

Create

Continue the magic,
Rise to the challenge,
Embark in a making,
Appearing from nothing
Through sheer power,
Emulating the Creator.

Endure

End of adversity
Nowhere in sight,
Dilemma and difficulty,
Unrelenting plight.
Remain abiding,
Emerge prevailing.

Flow

Frictionless motion
Lessen obstruction,
Onward fruition
With inspiration.

Focus

Fine-tune your attention
On the matter at hand,
Concentrate volition
Upon a single point,
Stray not from what's begun.

Forgive

From flaws, mistake,
Offense or hurt,
Release the heart.
Grieve not, grip not
Issues that rot
Vigor and strength,
Escape resentment.

Grow

Gain substance,
Reach greater heights,
Overcome hindrance,
Welcome new insights.

Heal

Health is hurt,
Energy low;
Allow rebirth,
Let love flow.

Hear

Heart prepared,
Ears open,
Always attentive,
Ready to listen.

Help

Hold out your hand to the struggling,
Elevate the forlorn from grief,
Lend your ears to the unheeded,
Protect the injured and weak.

Inspire

Ignite a passion,
Nudge a dream,
Support a person
Pursue his stream.
Illustrate a path,
Right the astray,
Example your way.

Know

Keep track of events,
Network with the adept,
Observe environment,
Wonder with enlightenment.

Laugh

Let loose a hearty sound,
Amuse in funny things,
Unleash the cheer once bound,
Gleefully receive good tidings,
Hilarious roar is healing.

Learn

Listen and discern,
Engage in concern,
Attain a knowing,
Realize meaning,
Nail understanding.

Plan

Provide a blueprint,
Lay strong foundation,
Anticipate requisites,
Necessitate strategem.

Praise

Pleased and delighted?
Reciprocate glee,
Admiration shared
Inspires positivity,
Spread jubilation
Enhances relation.

Pray

Perfect peace presides,
Request springs from soul,
Always placing trust,
Yonder Powerful of all.

Respect

Regard others
Equally as your own,
Sincerity matters,
Politeness and honor.
Embrace diversity,
Consider every entity,
Treat well their identity.

Save

Spend some income for your future,
Allot a part to pay yourself,
Vanish fears of looming fortune,
Economize to safeguard wealth.

Seek

Search actively,
Explore extensibly,
Expand from boundary,
Keep looking insistently.

Share

Spread the blessing,
Heartily dividing;
Abundance will shower,
Returning the favor
Expended to others.

Smile

Showcase that twinkle,
Merry, mirthful sparkle,
If curves be your asset,
Let your lips arch skyward,
Eyes bow like the rainbow.

Strive

Stay on course
Though sail is rough,
Reach for your goals,
Ignite your light,
Vigorously touch
Esteemed delight.

Succeed

Surrender to fate,

Unleash your might,

Cherish your state,

Continue the light

Emitted to date,

Extend what's bright,

Destined to great.

Thank

Through good and bad,
Happy and sad,
Always find aught
Noteworthy saught,
Kind, grateful thought.

Transcend

Traverse the veil,

Rise from the flames,

Above walls and limits.

Never allow

Scarcity and fear

Corrupt your tomorrow.

Eclipse the gloom,

Nadir and doom, when you're

Destined to bloom.

Trust

Throw yourself in free fall,
Rely in yourself and all
Universe commissions
Supporting your mission
Towards steady fruition.

Value

Very important
Above all desires,
Last to lose, first to want,
Understated worth,
Enormous regard.

Work

Waking up each day to do
Our contribution to the world,
Returning blessings back to who
Keenly does more than what was told.

Workship

Wonderful Father,
Omnipotent God,
Receive our prayers,
Songs of delight,
Hymns from our hearts,
Inspired by the Spirit,
Praise Your Holy Might!

Have

Hold your possession,
Acquire a treasure,
Victorious despite contention,
Experience sublime pleasure.

Abundance

Astounding state,
Blessedness shown,
Universe is template -
New stars are born.
Different lifeforms in
Astonishing array,
Needs furnished in spare.
Copious belongings,
Extraordinary blessings.

Awe

Amazing adventure,
Wonderful world,
Exciting life.

Beauty

Believe in your light -
Every star vibrates,
Attunes and delights
Uniquely on earth,
Turn heads and hearts to see
Your distinctive quality.

Courage

Confront your lament,
Overcome your limitation,
Understand your sentiment,
Respect your emotion.
Adapt to the environment,
Gain momentum, but
Expect battles to combat.

Discipline

Do your tasks faithfully,
In a timed and timely manner,
Spend each moment valuably,
Carefully attending to endeavor.
Instructions show correct way,
Principles guide the path,
Listen earnestly to counsel,
Instill pure teachings in your heart.
Nobly conduct your profession,
Embrace the guidelines for your mission.

Faith

Firmly believing in things unseen,
Adamant against deceiving
Impossibilities and despondency,
Trusting wholeheartedly in
Higher oath and ideology.

Family

Firmly rooted,

Able to grow,

Movement fostered,

Identity glow,

Love is conferred

Yesterday, today and tomorrow.

Freedom

From unhealthy attachments,
Release your heart and soul.
Escape entanglements,
Envision your goal.
Discover your worth,
Obey your true north,
Move out of your prison.

Friend

Founded on mutual trust,
Remaining in best and worst,
Identity respected,
Experiences shared,
Never-ending support,
Dependable comrade.

Glory

Great achievements,
Laudable endeavors,
Overcome obstacles,
Renowned with honor,
Yesteryears' splendor.

Grit

Grandiose goal
Require resolve;
Inexorably evolve,
Tenacious soul.

Harmony

Heavenly song,
Angelic tune,
Rhythmic throng,
Musical dune.
Opposite notes
Nonetheless denote
Yearning of souls.

Heart

Human life resides,
Every beat decides,
Affection whence ascribed,
Reflecting from inside,
Treasured trove that guides.

Home

Here is where
Ordinary men are kings,
Maids are queens,
Enveloped in love and care.

Hope

Heal all wounds the past inflicted,
Overcome each barrier present,
Perceive a future amid gloom,
Endure the pains and let life bloom.

Humor

Happiness is a gift,
Unwrap the funny twist
Merged in every plot,
Obviate a blot,
Replace with laugh.

Integrity

Incorruptible,

Nonnegotiable,

Tenacious,

Exemplary,

Genuine,

Righteous,

Indivisible,

Trustworthy,

Year after year after year.

Joy

Just living life in the moment,
One mind, heart, and soul in alignment,
Youthful in delight and excitement.

Legacy

Leave behind a lasting
Endowment to mankind.
Gift a portion of your heart
After it has long ceased to beat.
Continue to pass a torch the
Youth tomorrow will thank you for.

Light

Luminary -
Illuminating
Guiding,
Honing,
Teaching.

Life

Light dances with matter,
Ideas exchanged with neighbor,
Free the spirit to wander,
Enjoy each emotion with ardor.

Longevity

Live a long life
Overflowing with
Numerous wins.
Gain perspectives,
Experience the full
Vitality of being.
Instruct the youth
Through wisdom
You've gained in ages.

Love

Living life in bliss and laughter,
Overcoming obstacles together,
Victorious even in the worst disaster,
Everything is you that matter.

Mercy

Misdeed may cloud a connection,
Exceeding damp an affection,
Remorse stirs a reception,
Compassion erases upset,
Yesterday's offense to forget.

Mission

Make every day count.
Instill diligence,
Stamp your presence,
Succeed and mount
Into your calling.
Observe the guidance
Nudging your being.

Paradise

Palace beyond the skies,
Angels guard day and night,
Reigned by an Awesome Might,
Abundant grace supplied,
Diamond and golden tribe,
Infinitely bright,
Shining in stunning light,
Eternal love and life.

Peace

Prayerful and contented,
Even through difficulties,
Amid uncertainties,
Chaos, changes, and challenges,
Exists a calm untormented.

Prosperity

Positioned in a stable spot,
Resounding gain in every stake,
Official of the gifted craft,
Success is blessed each step he takes.
Possessions multiply with time,
Expanding like a yeasted dough,
Returning all the toils sublime,
Interests continue to grow.
Thriving, when the world is starved;
Yearning none, when fate is carved.

Serenity

Sweet slumber dwells
Even in the most disturbed,
Repose in chaos repels
Enemies dumbfounded,
Not expecting a smile
In return for an insult,
Try as the wind howl,
Yet calm still results.

Strength

Standing in the midst of storm,
Together deal with any gloom,
Remaining when all else has fled,
Erected though all vigor spent.
Notwithstanding all the hardship,
Grace is gained, empowered to keep,
Tough, trained, tested and entitled,
Hero's welcome truly deserved.

Temperance

To natural inclination,
Excitement and passion,
Maneuver with moderation.
Pass through situations
Exhibiting caution,
Restraint and restriction.
Abstain fom intoxication,
Negate addiction,
Control your volition,
Exude a conviction.

Victory

Valiantly we face the enemy,
Intelligently dealing with adversary,
Controlling compulsions,
Targeted efforts with direction,
Obeying supreme instruction,
Robed in weary jubilation,
Yomping to a celebration.

Vision

Visualize who and where you want to be,
Imagine alternate reality,
Space and time are yours to maneuver,
Infinite ways to make your life better,
Opportunities knock to those who dream
Never-ending upgrades await upstream.

Wisdom

When faced with forks on the road,

Irresolute choices spread,

Sound judgement is reached,

Dilemma deciphered,

Order restored,

Mind mastered.

About the Author

Rhodesia

Rhodesia has written poetry since the tender age of three, was once hailed as Philippines' Youngest Author at the age of nine, having compiled an anthology of poems. Her writing craft paused when she focused on clinical, academic, and administrative duties as a physician. Currently a devoted mother of two, she has rejuvenated her love for the written word.

www.ingramcontent.com/pod-product-compliance
Lightning Source LLC
LaVergne TN
LVHW041531070526
838199LV00046B/1615